T0129459

Embracing the Challenges of Change

Transitioning through Life through
the Challenges of Change

One Season to the Next

Kedric L. McKnight

authorHOUSE®

AuthorHouse™
1663 Liberty Drive
Bloomington, IN 47403
www.authorhouse.com
Phone: 1 (800) 839-8640

Published by AuthorHouse 11/20/2018

ISBN: 978-1-5462-6715-7 (sc)
ISBN: 978-1-5462-6714-0 (e)

Print information available on the last page.

This book is printed on acid-free paper.

Contents

This chapter is based upon both personal and third party experiences that have shaped my journey. It describes the spiritual, mental, emotional, and physical aspects of how pain is used to mold God's people into vessels fit to do ministry.

This chapter captures a view of Philippians 4:11 from a perspective of how we as believers face the various challenges of life. Whether it is divorce, financial duress, disappointment, racism, depression, inner struggles, etc. The basic theme is understanding how to maintain a level of contentment regardless of the circumstances.

This chapter explores the dimensions of God's grace. What is Grace? How does one receive Grace? Are we grandfathered into Grace?

This chapter speaks of how many people fail to maximize the limits of their faith.

This chapter discusses the importance of patience and how effective usage of patience during times of crisis, chaos, and confusion develop Christian character.

This chapter catalogues my journey as an African American man working within a racially bias and discriminatory environment. But, it details the spiritual coping mechanisms and the desire to make an impact as a trailblazer within an occupation that is vastly populated with whites. It speaks of my transition from Government Agent to Agent of God! It chronicles the good, the bad, and the ugly.

This chapter provides examples and statistics of why so many believers are "burned out" in traditional worship environments. It also explores various reasons why non-believers and church skeptics view modern day church goers as hypocrites, as well as Christianity as a hoax.

Acknowledgement

꠸

Spiritual inspiration, solid preparation, and sincere dedication are the three essential elements that I used in writing this book. I can honestly say that God has blessed me to publish my very first book. Wow! When I think of the seasons of life and all that they have been comprised of, I can only say, "Thank you, Lord, for the continuous journey!" Absolutely, none of this would be possible without my Lord and Savior, Jesus Christ! Christ has been the strength of my life and is truly the Author and Finisher of my faith.

I am eternally grateful to both of my parents, Lonnie and Ruth McKnight. Dad, you have demonstrated the purest form of how a godly man exemplifies faith amid troubling times. To my mother, who is the essence of grace, perseverance, and unconditional love. To Lonette, my sister, you are my sister and my friend. Thank you for encouraging me to never give up, but to keep my head up. To my brother-in-law and niece, I love you to the moon and back. To my first-born son, Kedric J. McKnight, you are the best side of me. Your humor, clever statements, and genuine love for me as your father has taken me further than you will ever imagine. To my youngest son, Karson. Your smile lights up my life and the trust that you place in me is second to none. I truly love both of you!

To Keith Clarkson, a man of few words but has demonstrated what it means to remain in the sacredness of matrimony. To Boderich Taylor and Harvey McDaniel. To Blake (my barber). Thanks for being there when I needed you the most. We are brothers for life. Thank you Eugene Coy III. Man, the long talks, patience, and great advice has uplifted me more than you know. To the Brothers of the Delta Theta Chapter of Alpha

Phi Alpha Fraternity, Incorporated, Texas Southern University, Houston, Texas. Russell, Bo, the Twins, Pastor Session, Ron, Lennon, Edric, Neal, and the LB's of Fall '92, and brothers of Fall '95, thank you for helping me gain a greater understanding of true brotherhood!

To the David W. Carter class of '91. I extend my love to everyone. Everyone played a role in my development and understanding of closeness. To Coach Charles Walton, you are like another father to me. You taught me what the meaning of having "grit" is all about. To Pastor Johnnie R. Bradley of the Shiloh Missionary Baptist Church. The blessing of our bond as brothers in the ministry means everything to me. Thank you for taking the time to encourage me, enlighten me, and to uplift me when I needed it. To Pastor James E. Mitchell, Sr. I am forever grateful for the wisdom you have provided me throughout the years. To my deceased grandmother, Mae Ola McKnight. Your kindness, comfort, and love will be with me until I see you in heaven. To my grandmother, Willie Mae Jackson. After 99 years of living, you are the epitome of God's grace. To Patricia A. Tucker, a woman who wears many hats. Thank you for demonstrating inner-strength and a spirit of never giving up. To the leaders and members of the New Mt. Calvary Baptist Church and New Life Bible Fellowship Church, thank you for entrusting the ministry of the gospel to me.

To Felecia Hunter-Burnett, you know how to be a friend indeed! Keith Hunt, thank you for showing me how to allow humor to minister to me. Ross Moore, you are an unsung hero among men. Finally, to my beautifully, authentic, calming, and Christ-centered blessing from God, Melissa. You are the best thing that has ever happened to me. Thank you for ALWAYS understanding and supporting me. You make me strive to be a better man daily. Your presence in my life is a constant reminder that if you wait on the Lord, a better season is sure to come.

Foreword

❦

Dr. Thomas W. Spann

The self-help book market is flooded with thousands of volumes that counsel how to rise from misery to a miracle. There is no doubt that many Christians have found solace in the messages contained in these motivational texts. Due to these massive missives on personal growth and self-service religiosity, it would be fair to ask the following question: Do we need more of the same, that is, a variation on an overworked theme? McKnight's book title hints at this indulgence; however, upon closer inspection, one is disabused of this prejudice. Certainly the title invites the mind to reflect upon the natural transitions of life. There are seasons of success, seasons of disappointment, seasons of childrearing, and seasons of having to let go of loved ones.

It is intriguing to reflect upon the fact that McKnight chooses the metaphor of seasons instead of the oft-used image of storms. Black preachers are famous for their homiletical articulations on the theme of life's storms. A popular dictum states: Either you are coming out of a storm, going through a storm, or headed into a storm. McKnight has selected a motif that shifts the reader's mind from the storms of life to the seasons of life. Seasons do not have to be thought of as radically disruptive or unexpected, though they may be. Seasons are organic, happenings in the flow of the human and natural life cycles.

McKnight's title invites reflection on the seasons of the reader's own life. As we know, seasons come and seasons go. Rarely are we fully the arbiters of determining the timing or the length of a season's duration. There is an impulse, a force, which moves with life itself that is responsible for the vitality and the transitoriness of life. Some refer to this power or force by various names. McKnight, writing from a faith perspective, would call this power or force, God.

I believe McKnight would acknowledge that the movement from one season to the next is not distinctive to Christian existence. Christian readers of this book, however, will be liberated from the myth that preachers or pastors do not go through the same troubles and tribulations as the rest of us. A lay person is looking through rosy or false lenses when the pastor is seen as standing above the narratives of strain and struggle.

McKnight is courageous enough to give his readers the lenses of authenticity, vulnerability, and transparency. Authenticity is a leader's best friend. By being vulnerable and transparent, McKnight opens the path for others—especially male leaders—to search for the door that would lead them on a similar journey. I can only conclude that it is now well with McKnight's soul. Writing this book was part of his healing process. To be well does not necessarily mean that there is now a worry-free soul. Fundamentally, it is well when the soul is surrendered to God who is the Strength of life and the Sustainer who holds us in perfect peace.

Now, McKnight could have compiled some of his sermons under the same title, and this book would still be a good read. He has not done that here. Instead, he combines autobiography, teaching, and preaching to move the reader with him to the next season.

For Christian educators and small group leaders who are looking for new material, please consider using this wonderful text.

I am confident that we have not heard the last from McKnight as a writer.

Introduction

✤

It goes without saying that most of us, if not all of us, find ourselves in a mode of reflection on a constant basis. However, I have found that reflection without purpose and objectivity is much like a notable statement that my dad uttered frequently when I was a teenager. He said, "Son, if a man doesn't have a purpose for doing anything in life, that's like going to a well and getting half a glass of water!" In other words, it's a colossal waste of time and effort.

With these soul stirring words, I began to reflect upon seasons of my life. I determined that transitioning from one season to the next season is not only necessary for personal growth, but it's so important in the evolution of faith cultivation. Thus, the basis of this book began to grow legs, first in my mind, then eventually in my heart. After a period of years, I have matured to a point where I can express many of my inward thoughts in somewhat of a memoir and autobiographical format. Interestingly, much of the content has derived from personal experiences, thoughts, or actual occurrences that I have witnessed or was privy to hear about.

Life has a funny way of certainly coming full circle. But, facing the challenges of change throughout various seasons of one's life is sometimes easier said than done. How does one cope with pain when it seems to be the only constant in your life? Is avoidance the key to surviving the pitfalls associated with the varied degrees of pain in life? Are any of your relationships unstable, unpredictable, and filled with a cycle of never ending twists and turns? If so, I discuss how one must embrace whatever you face. Ultimately, you will discover in your reading that Christ is the common denominator and the prevailing theme when things have gone relatively smoothly or when facing crisis and critical moments in life. It's through the grace and mercy that Christ provides us that we can stand in these perilous times.

The ability to leverage priceless lessons from prior occurrences can enable many to gain wisdom for our daily walk in this journey called life. As you read, ponder what has been written. Then, place yourself solely within my proverbial shoes. When you perform the above steps, I truly believe you will see my heart and understand in totality why it was important for me to write specific information within a chapter.

I would love to tell you that I have been mistake free in any one area of my life. But, this would simply not be true. But, as a child of God, this book allows one to acknowledge the humility and oneness that God expects from His children.

On one hand, I concur with the theory that the family that prays together will stay together. But, what happens when the bills are due, groceries are lack, paychecks are thinning, and filling up the gas tank in your car is almost costlier per gallon than a value meal served at McDonald's? Patience with the process is also a theme throughout this book. Relationships on any level take time to grow and most assuredly need nurturing. Whether in a church setting or at home, the need to employ patience is necessary in every aspect of life. This is especially true when one is employed in a bi-vocational capacity as a pastor and a federal agent. Have you ever exhausted yourself in ministry? The family takes a backseat while others in the ministry gain more quality time and attention from you. Yet, another challenge and change to explore. Yes, this dynamic presented loads of problems because of the obvious conflict of interests as it relates to the treatment of people and those small, yet robust intangibles called ethics and morals. So, to my fellow readers, grab a cup of coffee and a few of your favorite snacks. Enjoy the read...God speed!

Season 1

"As a matter of important distinction, pain in and of itself can only be matched by its ability to provoke persistence in one's psyche to proceed. For when pain is properly applied, the true-grit within one's self develops the ability to aspire and achieve despite the levels of fatigue and weariness that one faces throughout the trials and tribulations of life."

K.L. McKnight 2018

Pain is My Middle Name

☙

*"Surely, he took up our pain and bore our suffering, yet we considered him
punished by God, stricken by him and afflicted."*
Isaiah 53:4

How old is pain? From the very beginning, it's always been here. Pain
was sandwiched between pride and the promise of God when Lucifer's
downward spiral occurred. Pain reared its head in the Garden of Eden and
we find it lying between earthly decisions and eternal destiny. Pain shows
up in the layers of four hundred years of oppression, laced with bigotry
and beating, yet is countered by ancestral perseverance and benevolent
abolitionists.

Pain seizes the moment when the Atlanta child murders transpired
and is caught in a single glance when John F. Kennedy was assassinated.
Pain showed up when millions lost their lives in the Jewish Holocaust and
refused to take a backseat on September 11, 2001.

When a miscarriage occurs, that's pain. When "Pro-Choice" comes
amid the mental and the emotional thought processes of a woman and
an abortion is the imminent result, pain is "still birthed." When fireman
do all they can to save, yet smoke inhalation over-take the elderly person's
capacity to breathe, that's pain. When the inexorable EMT performs CPR
on the child for 45 minutes, but can't save the 7-year-old child, pain is not
only probable, it's incorrigible.

Pain showed up again on the neo-natal floor of St. Paul Hospital. But,
this time pain became bolder and more intrepid in its demeanor. Pain's
approach was as stealth as a carnivorous animal stalking its prey. But, it was
as subtle as a rainbow appearing after a storm has dissipated. Pain became

a formidable foe on October 14, 1972. Why? Because pain placed itself between the first and the last, the day that PAIN became my middle name.

Pressure Applied Is Necessary (P.A.I.N.)

When speaking to mothers from all walks of life, I have found numerous similarities when they reflect on pregnancy patterns, dietary desires, and even discussion about the future of an unborn child. However, what really stands out are the discussions of name selection.

Some of the most pivotal and intense discussions between expectant parents is the notion of name selection. Some parents desire their children to possess biblical names. Many choose ethnic names or names that hold cultural or historical significance, while others are more traditional and select children's names that reflect a generational namesake or a derivative of the family name. But, I dare say that I have yet to find one person, whether man or woman, who desires to name any of their children PAIN.

Even amidst the birthing of a child, no mother that I have spoken with has ever wished pain to be a part of their child's life in any shape, form, or fashion. After all, if names truly reflect an aura and platform of present and futuristic existence, then who in their right mind would knowingly project an image such as pain to the life of any innocent and unsuspecting child?

But, regardless of paternal desire or maternal instinct, experience has provided me evidence that pain is a necessary ingredient in the life of a human. As a matter of important distinction, pain in and of itself can only be matched by its ability to provoke persistence in one's psyche to proceed. For when pain is properly applied, the true-grit within one's self develops the ability to aspire, despite the levels of fatigue and weariness that one faces throughout the trials and tribulations of life.

In the immortal words of our Lord and Savior Jesus Christ, "These things have I spoken to you, that in Me you may have peace. In the world you will have tribulation, but be of good cheer, I have overcome the world." (John 16:33) When reading these words, several thoughts come into play.

These words convey a message that pain, discomfort, distress, and problems are simply a part of this life. These words also share an intent to foreshadow the issues of life and allows the believer to understand that the God we serve is not astonished, nor is He in amazement regarding the perils of this life and the certainty of the human's unavoidable fate regarding the impending hardships of this life.

But, to those who are reading this along with me, it imparts within all who trust in the name of Jesus, that we can have peace in the middle of problems. We can find comfort in the face of crisis. In fact, it challenges the believer to avoid acting Christ-less when one faces a Crisis! So, although we all share a commonality with pain being in the "middle" of our names, we can rest assured that Jesus has already overcome the world.

The Man

"Man that is born of a woman is of few days and full of trouble." Job 14:1

The existence of trouble encountered in my life has always been a revealing, yet menacing fact that has always rendered me perplexed. Job's account of mankind's existence is a compelling picture of a man's life seen through the lens of a God-fearing, faithful, consistently obedient man, who is faced with the unparalleled notion that regardless of his actions, trouble is and always will be a part of his life's legacy.

Since this is a biblical truth and a humanistic fact, it would appear that one could live life as recklessly and irresponsibly as deemed necessary and still possibly experience a similar outcome as one who was overly cautious, circumvented risk-taking, and made a conscious decision to live according to God's holy Word.

Well, the man pictured in the panoramic snapshot and personality of myself knows first-hand that the eventual outcome of one who lives life imprudently will eventually lead to self-inflicted hindrances and unnecessary heartache. The man inside of me has always wanted to have more, to be more, to live better, to strive for more, to achieve more, and not to settle for less. But, as I've grown in the grace of the Lord (this will be discussed in Chapter 3), I have a greater understanding regarding how pain is used to propel one's faith into an arena of sole dependence on the One who lived, bled, died, and rose again for every believer that shares the umbrella of Christianity with me.

3

It is this same belief that has now allowed me to not depend or trust in the mortal man's exasperating influence for which I am all too familiar. But, to learn to trust the spirit-filled man within me, who is desperate to lead the sometimes lonesome life of a man held in captivity by sin, yet has been released by the blood of Jesus to live a life destined for eternal greatness. But, who may never taste the level of coveted immensity longed for in this life.

As one who served and trained under the leadership of Rev. Larry J. Sanders, Sr., the Senior Pastor of Keller Springs Baptist Church in Carrolton, TX, I was introduced to a litany of poetic works.

In one of his pastoral mentor-to-mentee moments, Pastor Sanders introduced me to the timeless words of one of our nation's former political giants, Theodore Roosevelt. After reading Roosevelt's words, I adopted the ingenious and imaginative words of this historically significant leader when he was charismatically delivering a speech at the Sorbonne in Paris France.

Former President Roosevelt said, *"It is not the critic who counts; not the man who points out how the strong man stumbles, or where the doer of deeds could have done them better. The credit belongs to the man who is actually in the arena, whose face is marred by dust and sweat and blood; who strives valiantly; who errs, who comes short again and again, because there is no effort without error and shortcoming; but who does actually strive to do the deeds; who knows great enthusiasms, the great devotions; who spends himself in a worthy cause; who at the best knows in the end the triumph of high achievement, and who at the worst, if he fails, at least he fails while daring greatly, so that his place shall never be with those cold and timid souls who neither know victory nor defeat!"*

Undoubtedly, the man, Kedric Len McKnight, who was born in 1972, is flawed. Yes, Kedric has failed in relationships both professionally and personally. Yet, he has an acute desire to keep pressing, to keep striving, and to keep trying until his human body expels his last breath and the new man relieves his mortality to put on immortality as promised by our maker. Until that assigned appointment transpires, I have no doubt that this man will continue in the pursuit of his purpose, while never sacrificing the innate capacity to travel life's pathway with great fervor and passion.

The Mirror

Anyone who listens to the Word, but does not obey, it is like glancing at your face in a mirror; and after looking at himself, goes away and immediately forgets what he looks like. James 1:23-24

Let's be honest, it's not until after you have truly reflected on your life and all of your experiences that you're able to identify the effects of unwise choices, hasty decision making, and outcomes that you know directly resulted from lack of prayerful consideration.

On numerous occasions, I have found myself taking life's exams over and over again. In the sovereign will of God, I believe that He allows His children to engage in multiple re-tests in order for us to see our mistakes firsthand and to correct the issues that may have caused us pointless and preventable problems. However, when we learn the intended lesson, I have found that the lessons learned will not only enhance our need for the Holy Spirit's guidance, but the likelihood of increased spiritual maturity is plausible. In the words of a great friend, Sister Hunter-Burnett, "Life's bought lessons are life's taught lessons!"

So, what does the mirror show? It shows the transition from the boyish grin of earlier years. It captures the serious countenance of the here and now. It embraces the smile of completeness when thoughts of my two sons (Kedric and Karson) captivate the aura of my expressions. But, life also has an uncanny way of displaying the fatigue of a warrior that's been in battle for years, with few breaks, wounded with evident battle scars and laced with strength from enduring daily shots fired intended to eradicate him. So, what does the mirror reflect? It yields the by-products of enduring pain, but holding onto the promises of God, from one season to the next.

"Certainly, we could go on and on with countless scenarios about the pressures and problems that we all face. And with time, we may form a viable working group or committee of conversationalist that do nothing but waste time restating the obvious accepted norms of society and our culture. But, if we are to gain solutions to what has now become a common theme of believers to exercise ungratefulness and regular bouts of discontentment, which eventually translates into sinful choices within our homes, communities, and societies, we must turn to the Lord and see what the Word of God has to say about our current state."

K.L. McKnight 2018

Embrace What You Face

❦

"Not that I was ever in need, for I have learned how to be content with whatever I have." Philippians 4:11

Arrest my attention from the very beginning. Isolate my thoughts and place a spotlight on the object that has captured my concentration. This is one of the foremost aims of writing! As a reader of historical poetry, fictional and non-fictional writing, and vast amounts of literary works, the gamut of creative styles and conveyance of information from the author's viewpoint has always intrigued me. So, it is no wonder that English poet and playwright, Robert Browning, who was stated to be a master craftsman of dramatic monologues during the Victorian era enthralled me. Browning's timeless quote depicting pleasure and sorrow helped to form the basis for the writing of this chapter.

Browning said:

> *"I walked a mile with Pleasure; she chatted all the way;*
> *But left me none the wiser for all that she had to say.*
> *I walked a mile with Sorrow, and ne'er a word said she;*
> *But, Oh! The things I learned from her when Sorrow walked with me."*

"When the characterization of abstract thoughts is communicated in a manner such that the proposed recipient can grasp the true essence of the originator's intent, it is then that the birthing ground of wisdom and understanding can take place." *(K.L. McKnight 2018)*

It would be a complete fallacy to project an image on paper of a person that was naturally born to embrace every struggle, every challenge, every problem, every failure, and every flaw that this marathon called "Life" has so graciously pointed out to me. Through life experience, both in "lift-offs" and "let downs," I have found that the seasons of life are as speckled as the leaves on rosemary and as wide-ranging as the waves in the core of an ocean current. It is the intent, however, to share a modicum of my thoughts regarding how one is to embrace what you face.

Setbacks vs. Solutions

Let's deal with the probing question: How do you learn to embrace whatever you face without resisting the challenges of change? I know, you have a solution already, right? You've already solved the quandary of questions regarding embracing setbacks and the difficulties that come with life. But, how does a dark-skinned, black male from birth get used to being called Nigger? How does an aged and seasoned black woman formulate a tolerance for being called Gal? How does a hard-working woman, either married or unwed, with children or without, accept the name of "Bitch" when she wasn't born with it naturally?

It appears you have it all together. So, I'm guessing your response is something like: We recognize ignorance and shallow mindedness and rise above it with actions and unmatched integrity. Well, this sounds good and it's put together well. But, I have some news for you. Setbacks don't have a "one-size fits all" solution. Because how do people work for 20 years in an underappreciated career status, arrive to work early, stay at work late, work unpaid overtime from home, yet the results yield termination or forced resignation?

How do children embrace the separation and inevitable divorce of parents that were once stated to be "in-love," when the children did nothing to cause the parents to fall "out of love"? How does one stomach giving sacrifice after sacrifice in a monogamous relationship only to yield zero results? What is the solution for rearing your child in the ways of God, only to vividly watch your son or daughter intentionally choose a pathway that is destined for hell if they continue? Are we to simply embrace that?

Certainly, we could go on an on with countless scenarios about the pressures and problems that we all face. And with time, we may form a viable working group or committee of conversationalist that do nothing but waste time restating the obvious accepted norms of society and our culture. But, if we are to truly gain answers and solutions to what is now a common theme of neglect of being thankful, ungrateful, and discontentment—which translates into sinful choices within our homes, communities, and societies—we must turn to the Lord and see what the Word of God has to say about the state of our current situation.

2 Chronicles 7:14 states:

> *"If my people who are called by my name will humble themselves and pray and seek my face and turn from their wicked ways, I will hear from heaven and will forgive their sins and restore their land."*

Let's look at what causes many to fail to embrace the contentment of life. Conversely, what motivates other individuals to relegate themselves to a pattern of consistent praise and reverence to God for the opportunities that they have been given in this season of their lives?

The Adrenaline Addict

It would not be superficial or a far stretch of the imagination to conclude that many of society's combined sense of loyalty to employers and employees, spouses and families, church members, friends and associates has been misguided, misappropriated, and suffers from mistaken identity. For we have become so busy in our materialistic and fast paced individual lifestyles that we rarely make time to embrace anything or anyone that does not immediately impact our inner circle. This has aided our families and communities in suffering from a crisis of mistaken identity. The need strikes many individuals to search for the proverbial "quick rush" of success, while discounting all that we've been blessed to learn while striving to move from one season of our lives to the next. Discontentment has become the social norm in our world and rather than acknowledging a God desired spiritual state of peaceful contentment, many would rather work 2-3 jobs to satisfy the cravings of worldly things. This has become an unconscious, yet actionable offense. Why? Because this mentality speaks volumes regarding our departure from godly principles and our natural inability to handle the everchanging processes, pressures, and pains of life. We have become a society of adrenaline addicts with a "pill popping" mentality. Why do you think we take a pill for just about everything? We take pills to wake up, to go to sleep, to rest, to stop the pain, to make us more aware, and to calm us down. Most of this has been cultivated by a societal norm that it is normal to be stressed out. We then operate in a state of dysfunctional living because we have not learned to embrace being content in our current season. Please don't mistake peaceful contentment with personal complacency.

Being complacent can lead to stagnation and lack of spiritual and personal growth. However, contentment recognized and employed properly leads to stability in thoughts and actions. This invariably allows the individual experiencing this aspect of life to become more grateful and learn one of life's greatest lessons, and that is being thankful for what you have, because it could be worse. It is sad when modern day Christians that should focus on supernatural support with the assistance and guidance of the Holy Spirit would rather seek horoscopes, taro card readings, and other means of feeling comfortable with the knowledge of their current state. Therefore, many of these same individuals proceed in life with a diminished desire to seek a God that we say we can't see with the naked eye. This causes many to blindly seek sinful avenues to gain titles, worldly acceptance, "people ordained prominence," and self-reliant, self-seeking methods of achievement that eventually fades with this current age and time. We have not learned to embrace nor handle the hand that we have been dealt. We thrive on finding the next level in this life, while discounting the life we have been graciously given. This creates a natural adrenaline rush because it adds to our quest for our need to exist and belong in a temporary world with temporary time constraints attached to it. And when we don't get our desired rush when and how we want it, then the addictive nature of doing whatever it takes to survive kicks in. Even if it means stepping on someone, stabbing someone in the back, or selling our soul to get ahead. We do it to feed the adrenaline addict inside of us.

The "How To" of Embracing What You Are Facing

If we are to activate and apply the spiritually implied Pauline Principle of "being content" or embracing whatever season we are faced with in life, we must first learn to be honest within ourselves about our piercing desire to be more than what we are. This is a desire that is spiritually inbred. This is a desire that God wants for each of us. However, this process typically takes place in two stages.

The first stage is learning to "Seek the Kingdom of God and All of His Righteousness…" as stated in Matthew 6:33. The next stage of fully being able to quench the life-long desire to have more can and will only be fully realized in the "Perfected" spiritual state that will only take place after Christ makes His triumphant return.

This is very good news because God desires us to experience levels of abundance according to what He knows we can handle and embrace. God invariably knows what we need, how much we need, and when we need it. (Matthew 6:8) Understanding this principle will provide a greater understanding of His will for our lives and bring about the long awaited peaceful contentment that we routinely seek. So, if you truly want to learn and understand and experience the fulfillment of faith in action, and solve the conundrum of peaceful contentment, then learn how to embrace one day at a time, be thankful for your current position, and learn to walk in a consistent posture of gratefulness as you journey from one season to the next.

Season 2

"It is certain that Grace was present before the handles of time were formed or ever made known to you or myself. From a theological standpoint, Grace has been a part of our human existence from the inception of God's infinite design to make His people into the likeness of His image. In fact, Grace has not been described as a created source of any kind, but as a derivative God's love and mercy that has been given to us because God desires us to have it; not because we have done anything to deserve it."

K.L. McKnight 2018

The Genealogy of Grace

☙

"My grace is all you need. My power works best in weakness."
So now I am glad to boast about my weaknesses, so that the
power of Christ can work through me." 2 Corinthians 12:9

When you walk into a crowded room, or when you meet someone for the very first time, it is common courtesy and just good manners to introduce yourself to whomever you come into contact. At least that's how I was raised and reared. It could be argued that if the person walking into the area where people are present, that if no initiation of dialogue takes place, that person could be labeled as impolite, insolent, or ill-mannered. But, as I continue to experience the maturation process of growing into a more seasoned believer in Christ, I have found that Grace needs no introduction. Grace can never be mistaken for audacious, impertinent, or rude.

Grace is always a welcomed guest at the largest gathering or in small, quaint circles of fellowship. Grace is and should be the guest of honor at any occasion and is preferred to be the first to arrive and the last to depart. Grace has no visible companion, yet is accompanied by her renowned best friends, Love and Mercy, in all circumstances. Grace oftentimes has no words, yet speaks volumes simply with her mere presence. Yes, I have categorized Grace in a feminine tense because the evidence of reproductive capability is present anytime Grace appears. Grace, by description, can be used as a noun or a verb, and shares a multiplicity of definitions:

GRACE as a noun:

    A. simple elegance or refinement of movement.

    B. (in Christian belief) the free and unmerited favor of God, as manifested in the salvation of sinners and the bestowal of blessings.

Grace as a verb:

    A. do honor or credit to (someone or something) by one's presence.

It is certain that Grace was present before the handles of time were formed or ever made known to you or myself. From a theological standpoint, Grace has been a part of our human existence from the inception of God's infinite design to make His people into the likeness of His image. In fact, Grace has not been described as a created source of any kind, but as a derivative of God's love and mercy that has been given to us because God desires us to have it, not because we have done anything to deserve it. This is called, "God's unmerited favor."

I don't believe in luck or coincidences. It literally drives me crazy to see televised interviews of people who have escaped near death or would be tragic situations, only to hear them utter the proverbial words of, "I feel really lucky." This is certainly an issue that I have prayed to not become too judgmental regarding.

But humor me for a moment. How could you be in a car while driving under the influence of alcohol, fall asleep, hit a cement embankment, the car subsequently catches on fire, and then you walk away with no major injuries? I will tell you. It's called God's grace. You and I have certainly done absolutely, positively nothing to deserve God's grace. But, because God loves us so much, He consistently provides His grace to us even though we are undeserving.

Grace Giving Episodes of Life

Allow me to share a few things with you as you read and ponder what I refer to as, "Grace Giving Episodes of Life." In the early years of growing up in Dallas, Texas, my family and I initially resided in a small area known as Highland Hills. Before I go any further, please allow me to preface this by stating that my parents (Ruth and Lonnie McKnight) are and were very good parents in all the areas that matter. They provided me love, substance, and a value system that has taken positive root within me. This, along with God's grace, is why I am still alive today.

To say that Highland Hills in the 1970s and early 1980s was an area layered with crime infestation and pockets of violence in certain branches of the community would be a fairly accurate statement. As a young boy, I can recall seeing other young people smoking marijuana and carrying small baggies of a white, powdery substance that I later found out was cocaine on their person. Sure, I was approached on several occasions to either smoke marijuana or even to sell different types of drugs to make money. However, because of my rearing and the exposure to the gospel of Jesus Christ at an early age, Grace abound and I was able to make good choices during some of the greatest times of temptation. Although this may seem very simple and appears to be a normative in our current society, it is not and should not be regarded as a simple matter of making choice based upon our own merits. I truly believe that God's grace is all so sufficient. (2 Corinthians. 12:9)

There is nothing that I did or have done to warrant God's grace. By the acknowledgment of God's ever-present work in my life at an early age, this gave even more latitude for Him to move into every area of my life. By the age of twelve, we had moved to the Oak Cliff area of Dallas. Although we resided in a middle-class neighborhood and a much better school district, there were still opportunities to make decisions that could negatively impact my life.

I thank God for teachers such as Ada Garner, Anita Elliott, Coach Charles Walton, Coach Freddie James, Bobby Nevels, and host of other instructors, parents, and pastors, such as Rev. James Mitchell and the late Rev. Floyd D. Harris for helping to keep me on the correct path.

As the years progressed, the temptations of life grew stronger. Now, the drug of choice was alcohol and sex. This is certainly not the proudest moment of my life, but unfortunately, the enemy presents opportunities to many of us that appear justifiable and understandable. I would tell myself, *After all, I had been a straight A-student, a member of the National Honor Society, was recruited by Ivy League, NAIA schools and various Division I schools for potential football and academic scholarships, and received both a full athletic and academic scholarship to Texas Southern University in Houston, Texas.*

I kept saying to myself, *You've been pretty good and very consistent and haven't caused problems for your parents. Why don't you go ahead and take a little sip of alcohol and have sex? It's okay, right?* Wrong! These two combinations could have been the death of me, my life, and my career, had it not been for the grace of God.

I can recall one incident in college. I woke up to a phone call from my mother. She knew I had been drinking. She was so disgusted that she hung up the telephone. This was not only disrespectful to her, but I wasn't raised in this manner. I had a woman (whose name I cannot recall) lying next to me and a half empty bottle of Hennessey Cognac. I literally could not remember all the events of the night. But I vaguely recall one of my good friends (Alisha McGlawn), who is a member of Alpha Kappa Alpha Sorority, drove me home from a house party. Alisha made sure that several of my fraternity brothers from Alpha Phi Alpha Fraternity, Inc. ensured that I was secured in my apartment when she left. Grace showed up in the form of a friend and an agent of kindness and safety.

Now, I would need this same grace to be a mediator between myself and my mother as I attempted to straighten out the disrespectful manner in which I undoubtedly answered the telephone. To this day, I still don't know all that I said to my mother, but I now affectionately refer to her as, "Grace," because of how she has always been there for me, stitched up scratches from bicycle falls, bandaged cuts, and scrapes from little league football, wiped away countless tears, hugged many hopeless nights away, sacrificed on my behalf, loved me unconditionally, and always forgave me. If you want a snapshot of a human depiction of grace and a visual picture of poetry in motion, it would be my mother. I thank God for His Grace and the mother He gave me.

So, how does this look for you as a reader? Where has grace shown up in your life? I will provide you some assistance if you need it. If you are reading this and you have not accepted Jesus Christ as your Lord and Savior (Romans 10:9), then guess what? You have been living on God's grace for far too long. So, take advantage of this scripture and find "Grace" for yourself.

If you have ever been in a situation that you and only you know seemed impossible to get out of, then you have experienced grace. If you have been in the military, traveled overseas, driven a car, been on a plane or a train, then you have experienced grace. Why? Because grace has allowed you to experience the uncertainty of life and still live to tell about it.

There are many who have lost their lives, not because grace did not prevail, but because of the sovereign will of God. It was their time to complete this side of life. This is one of the primary reasons why you should not take grace for granted. By the mere fact that you are alive and can share your experiences with someone else and possibly provide the benefit of your wisdom and knowledge is a part of the grace that God provides each of us.

You see, God desires each of us to share the awesome personal testimony of how His Son, Jesus Christ, has affected your life. Each time we share His Son, I believe that more opportunities for grace to be demonstrated in your life will take place. So, take a moment, ponder, and pray this prayer of Grace:

> Oh Righteous, Holy and Loving God, I am intentionally taking time out to thank You and to praise You for Your unmerited favor and grace. I deserve to suffer and not to have survived many of life's encounters. But, because of Your grace, I am still here. Please allow me to never take Your grace for granted or to take credit for anything that You have done. My desire is that a never-ending circuit and continuous extension of Your grace will always be a part of the life You have given me. And as I journey from one season in my life to the next, please keep me aware of how loving, merciful, and kind You have been. And finally, I acknowledge that from the very beginning, my heritage, my culture, my life, and the miracles that have taken place is because of the Genealogy of Grace that You have made available for me through Your life, ministry, death, burial, and resurrection. It is in Jesus name I pray. Amen.

"In essence, 'flesh level faith' means that one's faith is sometimes consigned to only what you can see or what one feels he or she can still control. When this occurs, it is no longer within the realm of faith. It has now entered the dismal realm of unrestrained fear. Fear has a detrimental impact on faith. Faith and Fear cannot coexist simultaneously. One will always override the other. Fear's first cousin is called, 'Doubt.' When doubt exists within the believer's mind, then the heart has already been subjected to spiritual warfare that exists between faith and fear. I state this boldly because the Apostle Paul is adamant and unwavering in his writing to his understudy, and amanuensis, Timothy when he pens the statement, 'God has not given us the spirit of fear, but of power, love and a sound mind.'" (2 Timothy 1:7)

K.L. McKnight 2018

Flesh Level Faith

❦

*"It was good for me to be afflicted, so that I may
learn your decrees." Psalm 119:71*

I know what the Hebrew writer stated in Hebrews 11:1: "Faith is the substance of things hoped for, the evidence of things not seen." I am keenly aware of what Hebrews 11:6 states regarding the impossibility of pleasing God without faith and that as believers, we must believe that God is who He states He is and when we actively apply this biblical statement, the Word of God affirms that He rewards those that diligently seek Him. I have read these scriptures over and over, as I am sure many of you have as well. I have heard a wide array of teachings on the topic of faith and sat through countless seminars and sermons on this deep-seated, yet still surreptitious and puzzling topic. Yet, there are times when I experience what I must call, "faith-fleeting" days.

Let the truth be told, and if you are 100 percent honest with yourself and others, you experience lack-luster faith that sometimes only makes it to the surface level. Sometimes the challenges of life become so difficult and tedious that a person's faith only captures them initially at flesh level and seemingly lacks the strength to enter one's spiritual blood-stream. I have pondered what would happen if we handled life's eventual uncertainties with such a high level of faith that absolutely nothing could shake our Christian beliefs, and to worry at any level would fall into the abyss of the unknown.

But, like many of you, I don't see it happening on this side. There are people that I have heard utter the words, "I don't worry about anything!" This statement amazes me because it almost seems unnatural not to have feelings of worry about at least something in life. Don't get me wrong, I can totally relate to not being a worry wart. I would not classify myself as someone who presses the panic button at the first sign of turbulence in life. However, to state that I have no worries in life would be a total fabrication. Quite frankly, sometimes I subconsciously worry about my two young sons when they are not in my presence. There are occasions when I have a grave tendency to worry about issues relative to my financial future and even the status of my personal and professional life. But, since we are being blatantly honest, let me share something with you. If you are one that tends to camouflage your obviously existent worry by labeling it as being "overly concerned," then you are currently in a state of denial regarding your emotional and mental status.

In essence, "flesh level faith" means that one's faith is sometimes consigned to only what you can see or what one feels he or she can still control. When this occurs, it is no longer within the realm of faith. It has now entered the dismal realm of unrestrained fear. Fear has a detrimental impact on faith. Faith and fear cannot coexist simultaneously. One will always override the other. Fear's first cousin is "Doubt." When doubt exists within the believer's mind, the heart has already been subjected to spiritual warfare that exists between faith and fear.

I state this boldly because the Apostle Paul was adamant and unwavering in his writing to his understudy and amanuensis Timothy when he penned the statement, *"God has not given us the spirit of fear, but of power, love and a sound mind."* (2 Timothy 1:7) I believe the Apostle Paul knew that fear had such an impact in the believer's ability to actively walk in faith. Thus, Paul readily stated with great conviction that God did not give us fear.

This statement of confident assurance by Paul not only provides the believer with an understanding that since God did not give us fear, then God does not advocate, support, or condone fear in any form. But, it also reaffirms the spiritual fact that God provides all His people with the proper tools to eradicate fear, and they are power, love, and a sound mind. Knowing this should assist other believers to grasp hold of a confident faith that is solid and resolute. No longer should the uncertainty of worldly things shackle believers. But, believers should exercise the power that faith has provided each of us when we come face to face with situations that we are visibly uncertain of the outcome.

Oftentimes, one's faith becomes a periodic internal struggle. Therefore, I found myself researching the scripture to explore how some of God's chosen men exemplified extraordinary measures of faith. So, I looked at Abraham. Word to the wise, when you begin to make comparisons between yourself and those stated in scripture, be ready for a spiritual curve ball! One might agree that Abraham is an honored and recognized iconic, biblical figure. Therefore, when you look at Abraham's life and the essence of who he was as a man, a husband, and a leader, the question must arise regarding his faith as a follower of God.

Once again, the Hebrew writer clearly and concisely identified the biblical principle of faith in Hebrews 11:8. This scripture states that, "Abraham went out without knowing where he was going." In other words, Abraham was so connected to God in his personal fellowship that he trusted God's plan and provision for his life regardless of where God may have directed him. This validates that point that the kind of faith we as believers must have cannot be tied to our plans, but must be tied to a person. That person is Jesus Christ. This begs the question: how long have you been saved? How long have you truly been walking with God?

I have been saved for over 25 years and I can honestly say that I have only truly been walking with Him closely within the last eight years or the third portion of what I will refer to as my salvific years of serving and following Christ closely. Sometimes, God will take us on meandering pathways that seem senseless to us, but God knows exactly where He is taking us. Oftentimes, heartache is part of the journey. Heartbreak is part of the roadside wreckage. Death and sickness play roles in our faith-filled development process. But, trusting God during our pursuit of spiritual maturity is part of the process.

I can now say that in this season of my life, I thank God for the afflictions, because it has taught and continues to nurture me in the spiritual growth process. I am thankful for God allowing me to go through the relationship break-ups, the professional conundrums, and the painstaking process of identifying false friends. But, as time moves forward, the challenges of change become more prevalent. Time truly stands still for no one, and the believer's faith must be rooted in nothing less than Christ Jesus. Developing ones' faith takes place over time. There is no such thing as a quick fix to faith. We must learn to trust God and only Him. Mankind will fail us, but God never fails.

I am certain that many reading this have experienced some form of upheaval in life. Perhaps an unplanned pregnancy, an unanticipated job relocation, or career move. Maybe the marriage was not a faith move, but a feeling mood. Now, it has not gone as planned. We must all learn to bring our thoughts, desires, and proposed plans to the Lord first. Much of the reasons why our faith resides at surface level is because we only trust what we can see and what we have control over. And since we can't see God with the naked eye as we desire, we don't trust Him in all areas of our lives as we should. Do you trust God with your finances and your family? What if you were called to an assignment in one place, then, without much notice, God tells you to pack up, get in the car, and drive, and He will tell you what direction once your family is all packed up and you're in the vehicle? Wow is right! Not many people would sign up for that assignment. Well, the truth of the matter is that faith is just like this at times.

The following statement has been made for years, "Let your conscious be your guide." We cannot walk in total faith depending on our fleshly conscious. We must, in turn, depend totally on God to be our compass. Imagine the challenge of uprooting your family after being called in Ur, then off to Haran, and much later you finally make your destination in the land of Canaan. It took years for this transition to take place. Much like Abraham, God sometimes allows it to take years to go from one season of our lives to the next.

Listen, before you become a little unsettled in your thoughts and make statements like, "I can't do this," or "I am not equipped to change like this," Abraham's faith was not always at the level that it eventually progressed to. Abraham was an ordinary person like you and me. But, God specializes in taking the ordinary person and making his/her life extraordinary when we place our faith in Him. Just think about it. Many of our senseless worries could be eliminated if we trusted God enough to handle our lives for us. Sure, God has given us the freewill of making decisions and choices. But, if our choices are rooted in things that are not pleasing to God, then they are certain to backfire. They always do.

Faith in Christ Jesus our Lord is tantamount to a lifestyle that pleases God. Please allow me to challenge you to develop a new focus as it relates to faith. Cease from attempting to live up to someone else's idea of where and how your faith needs to be. Instead, try to focus on God's expectations regarding your faith. No two people were created the same. We all have specialized DNA that separates us from one another. God's desire for your life's path is different that it is for someone else. But, there is one thing that God wants from all of us. God desires to be the center of our faith and focus. The remarkable outcome of a faith rooted entirely in God and God alone is a life that is transformed from a superficial and shallow confidence in Christ, into a life of conviction and certainty that is free from "flesh level faith."

Season 3

"For without patience as one of the prime motivating factors in one's life, then an individual's faith would be dysfunctional and complacent at best. Without patience as a foundational virtue, doubt, division, and desolation would hinder one's hope. Without patience at the helm, love would be a desperate emotion that becomes self-destructive, self-righteous, and self-indulgent. Patience is truly the piercing, penetrator of people."

K.L. McKnight 2018

Patience – The Piercing Penetrator of People

⚜

"And let us not grow weary in well doing,
for in due season we will reap if we do not give up."
Galatians 6:9

If I were to ask you how rocks are formed, what would be your response? I suspect that you would give any number of retorts that range from explaining the complexities of the lithification process or even something as simple as when mud hardens because water ceases to exist within the mud, thus a rock is formed. Either way, most could arguably agree that rocks are typically associated with being rigid, firm, and restrictive in nature. Sure, research indicates that rocks fall into either one or three classifications—sedimentary, metamorphic, and igneous.

But, more importantly, the take away from this segment is that rocks are formed based upon two things. These things are none other than pressure and time. For the purposes of this chapter, I will not focus much on the scientific areas surrounding the three classifications of rocks as much as I will attempt to focus on the stages of how rocks are formed.

Of these three classifications, metamorphic rocks fascinate me the most. For it is within the metamorphic stage of rock formation that we begin to understand the process of rock formulation in general. Research indicates that rocks are created and destroyed in cycles.

Moreover, it is the rock cycle that provides invaluable information to us regarding the origin of rocks. As rocks are eventually formed, we can surmise that a rock is either within the initial formation process, the breaking down process, or the reformation process. These cycles are what I will use to introduce the virtue called, Patience. Let's think about it for a moment.

The book of James states, "But, let patience have her perfect work; that you may be perfect and entire, lacking nothing…" This process of patience having to work mirrors the first phase of the rock formation process. Conversely, the Apostle Paul used a more abstract method of introducing the readers of his heralded epistles to the virtue of patience. In 1 Corinthians 13:13, the Apostle Paul states, *"Three things will last forever: faith, hope, and love; and the greatest of these is love."* I truly believe that one of most overlooked and underrated portions of the underlined text is the invisible presence of patience.

For without patience as the motivating factor in one's life, an individual's faith would be dysfunctional and complacent at best. Without patience as a foundational virtue, doubt, division, and desolation would hinder one's hope. Without patience at the helm, love would be a desperate emotion that becomes self-destructive, self-righteous, and self-indulgent. Patience is truly the piercing, penetrator of people.

The Patience of Rock Formation

I shared earlier in this chapter that rocks formed through the metamorphic process fascinates me. The reason this concept and process intrigues me so much is because it virtually outlines the life of a maturing believer in Christ. For a believer to maintain an upward progression in their maturity in Christ, one must embrace each season of life with passion, purpose, and prayer. Life is seasonal, and the cycles of life will range from disappointment and desperation to joy and jubilation. However, there should be a cemented sense of rock formation within all who wear the banner of Christ. A sand mentality will not withstand the test of time.

It's been proven that mud alone will not maintain foundational stability. But fixed, dense, concrete rock will maintain its form and solidify any foundation. This invariably supports the words of our Lord and Savior Jesus Christ in the gospel of John 1:42: *"Your name is Simon, son of John— but you will be called Cephas" (which means "Peter").* The actual Greek interpretation of the name Peter is Petros, which means rock. Although Peter was far from being the "rock-like," disciple that he would one day become, it was in that moment that his reputation was cemented in the handles of time.

This is much like many of us. We are not what we will be, but we are all in the process of becoming what God desires us to be. Therefore, we must consistently continue shaping the rock called patience in our lives.

Patience is inevitably the penetrator and initiator of our transition from one season to the next. It takes patience to live in an unemployed status, suffer from financial strain, discomfort, and bounce between bouts of depression. It takes patience to live between the uncertainty of a medical exam and the eventuality of incoming test results. One must garner patience when waiting on the verdict from a jury that supposedly decides your fate.

An expectant mother goes into the process with knowledge that it will take at least nine months of patience before the blessing of birth arrives. Researchers and expert analysts must utilize patience as they anticipate and await scientific studies to be approved. It took patience for Christ to walk through each phase and every season of His life from birth, knowing that the inevitability of death by crucifixion would occur, with nails in each hand, spikes within his feet, a crown of thorns on His head, and Roman soldiers penetrating His sides through spear piercing. Yet, Jesus Christ remained patient, resilient, irrepressible and as the picture of courage while suffering on a criminal's cross for you and me.

Partnering with Patience

I can think of several concepts, ideas, principles, and beliefs that I would much rather collaborate with other than the likes of patience; because patience involves understanding the waiting process. If you're not inclined to wait, then you need to know that patience will test the very depth, height, and limits of your mental, emotional, and spiritual character. However, patience has something within its general make-up that begs the attention of all of us.

Patience contains the necessary ingredients for God's people to faithfully walk with Him. So, why not partner with patience? I think I know why. It has become a generally accepted practice for many to hurry up and make things happen. Most people currently do not want, like, or desire to engage in activity that forces them to activate or employ patience as a constant tool. Sure, many will become patient when and only when it is necessary.

But, the narrative for most mortals is, they do not like to wait. Fast food restaurants are notorious for testing our patience. Freeway traffic is another culprit in the constant vexation of partnering with patience. But, the benefits of engaging in a healthy partnership with patient practices far supersede the alternatives. Unfortunately, like many of us, I had to learn patience the hard way. After the demise of matrimonial relationships, career transition, sputtering church growth, health issues, and some financial woes, patience was the only thing silently clinging to my subconscious mind. There are times when I could hear patience saying to me, "I have been waiting for you to retain me and not just rent me for a day!" You see, patience is not a virtue that you can simply hang in the closet and collect dust. Patience is a necessary part of the believer's prayer arsenal and testimonial toolbox.

"You can either make patience your friend or
your adversary." (McKnight 2018)

Some of my greatest failures and significant successes were rooted in the heart of patience. When you don't know the outcome, lady patience is your best friend. Lady patience is not one who is concerned with being used because she is equipped with a limitless source of sovereignty. When lady patience is not used wisely, she can be a painful reminder of your blunders. When persistence has run its course, and knowledge has lost its merit, it is then that patience demonstrates how formidable she is. The virtue of patience has proven repeatedly to be a beneficial defense against the unpredictable presence of uncertainty. Therefore, use her often and use her well.

Employing patience during each season of your life will not only assist you with not underappreciating the value of each moment in life, but it will provide you with wisdom and understanding regarding when and how much patience to utilize in any given situation. So, my friend, when you deliberate over a major decision, but don't quite seem satisfied that you have found the solution, mediate on the Word of God, begin the process of partnering patience, and then remember what King David said: *"Wait on the Lord and be of good courage and He shall strengthen your heart. Again, I said, Wait."* (Psalm 27:14)

"Who was I to think that I could simply go back to business as usual in a workplace that was littered with haters, pretenders, and character assault experts? I was an African-American male, federal agent working for the United States Government. I was educated both in life experience and the hallowed walls of academia. I had common sense, book sense and now a sense of urgency towards the ministry for which I had been called. This type of career is and of itself an assignment fit only for the strong and not the weak or faint at heart. I received attacks from red-neck supervisors and management that were disguised during the day as government workers, but I suspect, were really under-cover Ku Klux Klan members and imps dispatched by Satan himself."

K.L. McKnight 2018

From the Government to the Gospel

☙

"Do not fret because of evildoers, and be not envious against the workers of iniquity; for they will soon be cut off like grass and wither like the green herb." Psalm 37:1-2

There is a famous quote by Oliver Wendell Holmes that says, *"The real religion in the world comes from women much more than men; from mothers most of all, who carry the key to our souls in their bosoms."* To this very day, I believe this quote. It carries a large amount of weight because of the futuristic implications it presented in my life. My mother once told me that if I lived to be 21 years old, I would be a preacher. Of course, this is not something that a 12 year old wants to hear after a long day of going to school, doing homework, cleaning your room, and taking out the garbage. But, my mother assured me that God had placed this on her heart to tell me. After a few hours of pondering what my mother said to me, I wasn't as concerned with the immediacy of the possibility of preaching. I was more concerned with the, "If I lived to be 21 years old" statement. After all, is God not a God of certainty? Or was this simply a Freudian slip of the tongue by my mother in hopes that I would really take her words and statement to heart? Well, to this day, I still don't know and never really went back to ask. All I can tell you is that until I reached age 21, each birthday was as fun-filled as the law allowed. I took one day at a time and lived life to the fullest. Most importantly, I really learned at an early age to "number my days according to wisdom." Psalm 90:12

The Early Years

It was never my intention to become a preacher, much less a pastor. In fact, I did everything in my power and certainly within the fleshly part of me to deny the "calling" of the gospel proclamation upon my life. I guess I wanted to do like many people and just live what is termed as a "normal" life. I wanted to still go out drinking with friends at the Happy Hours. I wanted to still do things that I knew were far from society's view of what a preacher should engage in. I wanted to come and go as I pleased with no readily visible accountability measures.

After all, I have been structured most of my life. My dad is retired military. My mother was a probation officer. I had to be structured and focused in school. I had to maintain politeness in all other arenas of life. When I played football, I had to run between the hashmarks and even when I drive, I must stay within the lanes. I was finally tired of just doing everything by the book. I wanted to just "do me," if there is such a thing. Why would I ever embrace ministry from the preaching standpoint? Was it not good enough for me to participate in regular church worship service? Why is it that I can't come to church and simply leave and go home after hearing a message from the pastor?

The life of a preacher was certainly not for me, so I thought. I always wanted to be in federal law enforcement as a federal agent for the United States government. That was my career path and desire. When once asked about what I wanted for my future, becoming a preacher was not on the five-year plan of action for my life. Let's face it. Most of my prior personal encounters with ministers were rather dry and lacked appeal. Ministers appeared to live a very closed off life that lacked fun, excitement, and spontaneity.

Those adjectives describe a large part of my personality. Therefore, how could I ever think of being one of those preachers? Little did I know that God had a plan for me in this capacity all along. (Jeremiah 29:11) Until this day, I am convinced that God has an amazing sense of humor regarding His creation.

The Transition

And then it began. I know you're probably saying to yourself, "What is it that began?" I cannot tell you the number of times that I had dreams of me preaching to large masses of people. Then, if the dreams were not interrupting my once consistent sleep life, there were real life visions of things that would appear to me while I was at my house alone. As these occurrences began to take place, I attempted to discount them and minimize the impact they were having on my life. But, please understand me when I say this. God will not allow any of His plans to be thwarted. (Job 42:2)

Oftentimes, many ministers, including myself, have been guilty of making the ill-advised statement of, "I ran from God a long time." Although this is a true statement that mirrors the picture of Jonah, it is certainly not a statement to be proud of, to take pride in, and to marginalize the power of. This statement alone, and the disobedient actions that followed these words, is the very reason that I experienced an overwhelming, unexplained medical diagnosis of temporary physical paralysis. Thank God my paralysis was relatively a short period of time. But once I surrendered to the Voice, the Hand, and the Call of God to preach and proclaim the gospel of His Son, Jesus Christ on January 31, 2001, I began to immediately observe a positive transition in both my physical condition and spiritual position.

The Neighborhood of Negativity

Years ago, I read a quote that stuck with me. The quote stated, *Your life is not yours if you constantly care what others think.* Besides prayer and a great deal of restraint, I used this quote as a catalyst to get through the infamous "Neighborhood of Negativity."

"Please know that when you have the courage to accept, shoulder and embrace the challenges of change in your life, prepare to visibly observe and withstand the disquieted, doubting faction of people who question the authenticity of God's call on your life." (McKnight 2018)

Who was I to think that I could simply go back to business as usual in a workplace that was littered with haters, pretenders, and character assault experts? I was an African-American male, federal agent working for the United States Government. I was educated both in life experience and the hallowed walls of academia. I had common sense, book sense, and now a sense of urgency towards the ministry for which I had been called. This type of career is and of itself an assignment fit only for the strong and not the weak or faint at heart. I received attacks from red-neck supervisors and management that were disguised during the day as government workers, but I suspect were really undercover Ku Klux Klan members and imps dispatched by Satan himself. But, the worst attacks of all came from both women and men that share the same color of my skin and claim the exact same residue compiled from years of slave-mentality build up. This simply means, although blacks were supposedly declared free in 1863 via the Emancipation Proclamation, many of the mentalities and mindsets of my race-related counterparts within the workplace were still in bondage.

I had not seen more "cut-throats" within an organization until I was employed by the federal government in the capacity of law enforcement. It seemed like a professional nightmare began in my life after I accepted my calling to the gospel ministry. Prior to my acceptance of God's plan for me to preach, I believed things were good in my life professionally. I was able to fly under the radar and go relatively unnoticed by those individuals that I knew could possibly cause waves for me within my department.

But, without any true sign or alert, I began to receive unfair treatment regarding casework, a plethora of unreasonable work-related expectations, racially charged and targeted "in-house" investigations, undesirable assignments, only to be matched by leadership in most cases that lacked any sense of sound cerebral decision-making ability. It was then that I found out my life was truly transitioning into a new direction. This was totally un-familiar territory. My good friends, Keith and Eugene, once told me they were not surprised by the calling on my life. However, I really didn't take it to heart until they demonstrated their tremendous support, not as long-time friends, but as men that listened to what they termed as "God speaking through me."

I remember preaching my first sermon. Although, there were huge scores of people in attendance, I really didn't have as much third-party support as I imagined. Many of the people came as rubber-necking spectators who were simply watching an event take place. But, my immediate family has always been an incredible source of unrelenting support. My sister, Lonette, was enormously supportive because she said that she could see the transition taking place within me right before her eyes. Many of my close peers seemed to be genuinely supportive as well.

But, the government side of the house was sketchy, to say the least. How was I to balance the identity of being a federal agent and become a preacher of the gospel? I then developed nicknames such as pistol-packing-preacher and double agent McKnight. Wow! I asked God on numerous occasions whether this is truly my assignment, or did I misinterpret the call? The answer came so clearly from God. He said, "No, you have been positioned and purposed for this!" Now, there was no running at all. I had no choice but to accept the assignment regardless of the ridicule and the relentless pursuit of doubters who questioned both my commitment and my calling. How was I going to journey from the government to the gospel?

Spousal Support

The maturation process of going from living life on the "ledge of law-enforcement" to a life seemingly filled with "lanes of limitation" is not a garden variety assignment. This transition was not the most appealing aspect of my ongoing career that now suddenly involved a life laced with ministry. But, there was hope, right? After all, my spouse was there to support me, correct? To say, that the support was not there would not be entirely accurate. I had periodic spousal support emotionally on days that the plantation owners, who were my managers, were unbearable. I especially had support when I was involved in a shooting incident while working as part of a joint drug and violent crime task-force. I must say that when I needed to be away from home and the kids, I was reasonably supported in this capacity as well. I even had periodic prayer-based support from close friends, family and sometimes, total strangers.

It's been said that in life, there are no guarantees. This certainly was proven to be true in the case of my relationship. The only things supposedly certain are death and taxes! Well, having a marriage that withstood the tests of time and was able to weather any storm is not an accolade that I can add to the list of positive accomplishments in my lifetime. However, I can add it to a laundry list of things that I have in the category of "experienced deficiencies."

I can honestly admit with clarity and conviction that I understand what the late, great Langston Hughes meant when he poetically penned the timeless words of the ageless poem,

Mother to Son:

> *Life for me ain't been no crystal stair. It's had tacks in it and splinters and boards torn up; even places where there ain't been no carpet on the floor... Bare! But all the time I'se been a-climbin' on, and reachin' landin's, and turnin' corners, and sometimes goin' in the dark where there ain't been no light. So boy, don't you turn back. Don't you set down on the steps 'Cause you finds it's kinder hard. Don't you fall now—For I'se still goin', honey, I'se still climbin', And life for me ain't been no crystal stair.*

The things that I thought I needed and could depend on the most had now abruptly gone away. I found out that during this transition, a marriage that I once regarded as being secure and steady was now a marriage that was as safe and secure as those passengers aboard the Hindenburg or the Titanic. A very successful career now wreaked the odor of my decision to depart for personal reasons. Note, that this was an abrupt departure that was initiated based on severe marriage instability, a workplace lined with racial injustice, and a black female supervisor that deserved an Oscar for her best impressions of a 21st century version of Benedict Arnold, Julius Caesar's Brutus, and Mata Hari.

Until recently, I didn't quite understand the full gamut of targeted attacks towards me by those in leadership, who managed me while in transition from the government to the gospel. On one occasion, I was stated to have been engaged in ministry work while on duty. However, this was totally inaccurate. A racist supervisor was surfing the internet and found a radio station that was broadcasting a sermon that I preached two years prior to the date that he heard this sermon being rebroadcast. But, after reading John 15, I now understand with much more clarity the nature of the attacks and why I had to experience so much antagonism, disappointment, and loss. Jesus said, *"If the world hates you, remember that it hated me first. The world would love you as one of its own if you belonged to it, but you are no longer part of the world. I chose you to come out of the world, so it hates you."* (John 15:18-19)

Season 4

"When asked why church attendance apparently seems to be on the decline, personal testimonies of sadness, hurt, hypocrisy, damaged emotions, anger, resentment, and a host of other emotions came to the forefront. All too often, this happens to members within the body of Christ. When bible toting, scripture reading, true to heart Christian parishioners undergo such a negative experience from a place that was once a huge spiritual priority to them, it can cause them to develop a condition that I would like to refer to as: Spiritual Bankruptcy. A Christian, who becomes bankrupt in their belief system regarding the modern-day church, can be hazardous to the inner workings of church ministry and negatively impact evangelism efforts."

K.L. McKnight 2018

Bankrupt Believers

꤬

*"Come to Me, all who are weary and heavy-laden, and I will give you
rest. "Take My yoke upon you and learn from Me, for I am gentle and
humble in heart, and YOU WILL FIND REST FOR YOUR SOULS.
"For My yoke is easy and My burden is light." Matthew 11:28-30*

A study of recent statistics has revealed a staggering decline in church attendance
all over the country. Church attendance experts state that many people only
average a total of attending worship two Sundays per month. Millennials have
reportedly declined in regular attendance by approximately 59 percent. When
asked why church attendance apparently seems to be on the decline, personal
testimonies of sadness, hypocrisy, hurt, damaged emotions, anger, resentment,
and a host of other emotions came to the forefront. This brewing reality
has prompted me to discuss the seasonal transitions of church attendance,
the challenges of one's personal faith and overall spiritual commitment to
Christ. The below scenario is a fictional depiction, utilizing fictitious names
to indicate the portrayal of events personally witnessed by me or incidents
described to me by reliable third parties.

Mr. and Mrs. Faithful have been members of the Believe I'm Saved
Bible Church for many years. The Faithful family are consistent in bible
study, attend church worship services weekly, and frequently volunteer
for churchwide events. The Faithful family provides generous financial
love offerings to their pastor; they give well over the minimum 10 percent
tithes and offering and are avid grace givers to the "Hope we build a new
church" building fund. One day the Faithful family fell on hard times.
They desperately asked the church to assist them with their light bill until
the end of the current month. With no thought or deliberation, the church
trustees denied the Faithful family's request with no explanation.

As a result, the Faithful family was unimaginably hurt and disappointed. After prayer and much consideration, the Faithful family left the church wounded by the denial of their request for financial assistance. The Faithful family has not joined another church assembly since their experience in their previous church. The Faithful family was stated to have said, *"We never want to experience this type of hurt again. There was a total collapse in communication and the disregard of a real need displayed to our family that we did not matter. This was a slap in the face and we feel as though our years of service meant nothing."*

As a result, this family does not attend organized worship services and avoid what they term as the "political hierarchy of the church."

What happened? Why did an instantaneous level of tension rush through your veins as you read this? Did the Faithful family make the right decision in leaving the church? Was this simply the end of the Faithful family's season? After all, the Faithful family had a long history of being loyal and committed to this church assembly. In fact, if there were such a thing as a church membership prototype, the Faithful family had been the model church family in words, deeds, and actions. But, when the Faithful family needed the church ministry the most, the church declined to assist the family. To add insult to injury, there was no reason communicated regarding why the declination took place. The operative question is: Who was the final decision maker? Was the Faithful family simply a number within an assembly of other churchgoers? Was their request given serious consideration? Was the pastor of the church even informed? All too often, this happens to members within the body of Christ.

Moreover, when bible toting, scripture reading, true to heart Christian parishioners undergo such a negative experience from a place that was once a huge spiritual priority to them, it can cause them to develop a condition that I would like to refer to as *Spiritual Bankruptcy*. I wholeheartedly believe that a Christian who becomes bankrupt in their belief system regarding modern-day church practices, can be hazardous to the inner workings of church ministry and negatively impact evangelism efforts.

Definition: Bankruptcy * The state of experiencing a collapse, ruin, or failure.

Definition: Christian Believer * The act of having total trust and dependency in God or the things of God.

Definition: Bankrupt Believer * A Christian who has experienced a temporary or indefinite collapse in trust or dependency regarding the things of God.

What is causing bankruptcy in your ministry belief system? Have you been hurt by the same church under a different name? Was it a parishioner, pastor, or both? When did you first start experiencing feelings of uncertainty about your primary place of worship? Did you pray? Did you receive an answer? Do you feel that the church turned on you? Or was it you that actually turned on the church? These are questions that beg the enactment of self-examination.

As a father, a son, a brother, and a bi-vocational pastor, it is apparent that I wear many hats. But, sadly enough, I too, have experienced this dreadful condition of having feelings of being a bankrupt believer. Suffice it to say, ministry is hard work, but it can be extremely rewarding. Prior to accepting my call to the gospel ministry, I would never have equated church ministry as a breeding ground for harsh ridicule, a hub for hypocrisy, a concourse for gossip, or a vineyard of violence. I guess I didn't think my experiences would ever be so tantamount to those experienced by biblical iconic names such as the Apostle Paul, Peter, or Joseph.

But, the sad commentary is that many of my experiences right here in the Dallas/Ft. Worth, Texas area have emulated the unsympathetic, callous, and ruthless actions that took place in what many bible readers have examined within the pages of the bible. Believe it or not, ministry can hurt! I have experienced renegade and rebellious Deacons disrespecting me as their pastor. I have undergone the discomfort and dissatisfaction of being called to a church, only to have members of that assembly to blatantly disrespect me in front of my son. I have been falsely maligned, slandered, and denigrated as minister who used my calling as an excuse to coerce and manipulate others to follow my leadership. And in the most sincere efforts to serve and assist others, I have even been accused by those who I believed were close to me of finagling the female flock. If anything will cause you to become bankrupt in your belief system, try stomaching, sustaining, and standing while undergoing a series of attempted "character assassinations!"

But, through all of the muck, the mud, and the mess that oftentimes filters into the pond of parishioners, I have never totally lost sight of the awesome fact that God called me to this work. God anointed me for this work. God appointed me for this work. And God has intentionally positioned me as one of His earthly assigned preachers and pastors to proclaim the redemptive power of His Son, Jesus the Christ! And it is this same God who I have totally given my trust and allegiance to. Yes, when the vicissitudes of life bombard you, and they will, one has to remember that it is Jesus Christ who will keep you during times of doubt, indecision, and personal insecurity.

The Unparalleled Work of Christ

"It is virtually impossible for any individual to truly take a position as being a true believer in Christ and not have experienced the cold blade of betrayal by members within the body of Christ." The Apostle Paul shares one of his innermost feelings regarding the unparalleled work of Christ within him as man, an apostle, and ultimately a servant of God. On the heels of statements written in Philippians 3:7-9, the Apostle Paul shares that his greatest testament is not found in his earthy accomplishments, knowledge, or the high regards and esteem of mankind. No, the Apostle attributes his greatest work and labor in his life to that of the marvelous work of Christ within him. Paul's implicit testimony regarding the righteousness he has received through his faith in Christ alone is what staggered and stunned me in my very stance as I read. Paul identifies that he could literally have chosen the route of "righteous indignation" because of all that he has experienced and been exposed to in his walk with Christ.

Paul could have certainly boasted about his fluency in different languages, his Roman political savvy, or his epic encounters with men and women who actually walked with Christ and participated in Christ's earthly ministry. But, the Apostle took an entirely different stance. He attributed the most challenging times in ministry, the agonizing torture and abuse of himself, and even the betrayal of him by those closest to him as spiritual mile-markers that pointed towards a greater relationship with Christ. Paul was adamant that the believer must choose to formulate a single-minded viewpoint towards pressure and pain in life. Paul, even more than many of us, had every reason in the world to "take a spiritual break" from the rigors of ministry, which has been a constant for him. But, no, Paul said the reason he continued to minister despite threats of physical violence, imprisonment, or death; the reason he didn't allow spiritual burn out to occur; the reason he didn't allow trials and tribulations to corrupt his sensibility and initiate a mindset of spiritual bankruptcy is simply this:

Philippians 3:10: "That I may know Him and the power of His resurrection, and the fellowship of His sufferings, being made conformable to His death, if, by any means, I may attain to the resurrection from the dead."

This was the Apostle Paul's plea and frankly it should be the adopted motto of Christian faith within the believer. We, who are believers, should frame our faith within the unparalleled inner workings of Christ within us. When we go through the fiery darts of life and experience the tragedy of trials, tribulations, and temptations in life, we should remind ourselves that this is all so that "We may know Christ and become closer in fellowship with Him." That it is in times of our personal crisis, that we refuse to take a crippling stance of appearing Christ-less!

It is within the dampness of our tears and the cloak of darkness, disappointing, and depressing times that we emerge with the visible embrace for our invisible crosses to bear. Because it is only when we experience these seasons of our lives, my friends, that we truly begin to look like Christ.

I read a rousing and stirring quote on a Christian website one day. It stated, *If being hurt by church causes you to lose faith in God, then your faith was never really in God. Your faith was in people, not God!* Such a thought-provoking, yet simplistic statement. As I consider the things that I have faced in life, I am reminded that there is one additional season that many of us overlook. It's called "Due Season." The Holy Spirit, inspired writing of the Apostle Paul, never ceases to amaze me. In Galatians 6:9, it challenges believers not to allow exhaustion to overtake us, because in our "due season," we will gather a harvest of God's intentional blessings if we don't give up! This reassures me that Paul got it! He really knew what was around the corner of life. Paul knew what grandmother knew, that "trouble doesn't last always!" To all the people who have been bankrupt in your belief system, bankrupt in your pattern of thoughts, and experienced the bankruptcy of depleted relationships, hang in there. Help is on the way. God has promised to restore all of us in due season. I'm convinced now, more than ever, that as you experience life in its sometimes complex and complicated forms, choose to embrace life and take God with you from one season to the next.

Prayer is the necessity of all those who desire a close-knit fellowship with God through Christ Jesus. Prayer is the lifeline by which all believers use as a conduit of communication with Christ. Without it, nothing is possible. But, with it, all things are possible unto those who believe! Should our prayers be filled with lengthy requests of personal gain? Should our prayers be focused on the next blessing that we expect God to send our way? No, prayer should be direct, concise, intentional, and filled with thanksgiving and honor to whom it is due. Those who utilize prayer effectively will reap the benefits of a long-lasting relationship with Christ.

A Prayer to Ponder

✠

Oh, Lord, how magnificent is Your name! Thank You for your precious Son, Jesus Christ. During every season of my life You have been with me. When life seemed unbearable and there appeared to be no solution in sight, You were there. When the vicissitudes of life cause us, who are mortals to waver in areas that we shouldn't, it is You that reminds us to never lean to our own understanding, but to acknowledge You in everything and the direction to our paths will be made known.

God, I thank You for the various seasons of my life. It has molded me, shaped me, and alas, it has humbled me in ways that nothing else could. If it were not for the troubling times of crisis and moments of uncertainty, I would not truly understand how You know precisely how to soothe and solve situations with ease. Thank You, Father, for your goodness, grace, faithfulness, and your mercy.

As, I embark upon yet another season in life, please provide me with the fortitude and faithfulness needed to withstand the craftiness and the cunning ploys of the enemy. Lord, You have truly been a provider of protection and hope. It is with this same heavenly hope that I now have confidence and courage to face the seasons of life. Overshadow me, Lord, with an unparalleled approach to living life with intentional praise and acknowledgement of You.

Lord, my heart and my mind are open for You to fully control. Let the seasons of my life be faithful and fruitful so that You and You alone will receive all the glory and honor that You richly deserve. It is in the Matchless Name of Jesus Christ, I pray. Amen.

Points To Ponder

꧁

As you observe the seasons of life in their purest forms, you will begin to see that no season remains the same. Yes, my friends, all things change—the constant evolution of transitioning from childhood to adolescence, then from young adulthood to embracing the platform of being middle-aged. Then, alas, there is the season of winter in which many begin to reflect on the age-old experiences that embody all who have traveled this meandering pathway called life.

Well, One Season to the Next unveils new perspectives regarding how to find a spiritual balance during the constant transitions of life. This book is concise and succinct in its approach regarding how individuals should embrace the various challenges that life brings about. But more importantly, it describes how often grace is misrepresented as simply luck and how believers in Christ should truly thank God for his amazing grace. The author's intention is to convey a real-life message of how obstacles can serve as catalysts for spiritual transformation. This book provides a front-row seat into the life of one who has experienced great successes laced with great challenges.

Printed in the United States
By Bookmasters